a special gift for

_____

with love,

_____

_____

date

God knows and is interested both in the hardest problems we face and the tiniest details that concern us. He knows how to put everything in place, like a jigsaw puzzle, to make a beautiful picture.

Corrie ten Boom

hugs ™

Stories, sayings, and Scriptures to Encourage and Inspire

for women on the go

STEPHANIE HOWARD

Personalized Scriptures by
LEANN WEISS

HOWARD
PUBLISHING CO.

Our purpose at Howard Publishing is to:

- *Increase faith* in the hearts of growing Christians
- *Inspire holiness* in the lives of believers
- *Instill hope* in the hearts of struggling people everywhere

Because He's coming again!

Hugs for Women on the Go © 2002 by Stephanie Howard
All rights reserved. Printed in the United States of America
Published by Howard Publishing Co., Inc.
3117 North 7th Street, West Monroe, LA 71291-2227

05 06 07 08 09 10 11   10 9 8 7 6

Paraphrased Scriptures © 2001 LeAnn Weiss, 3006 Brandywine Dr.
Orlando, FL 32806; 407-898-4410

Edited by Dawn M. Brandon
Interior design by Stephanie Denney
Illustrations by LinDee Loveland

Library of Congress Cataloging-in-Publication Data

Lynne, Stephanie, 1974-
    Hugs for women on the go : stories, sayings, and scriptures to encourage and inspire /
Stephanie Howard ; personalized scriptures by LeAnn Weiss.
        p. cm.
    ISBN: 1-58229-265-5
    1. Christian women—Religious life. I. Weiss, LeAnn. II. Title.

BV4527 .L96 2002
242'.643—dc21   2002068810

contents

chapter one

you are effective

When you feel overwhelmed
and out of balance,
look up and remember
that your help comes from Me.
I've raised you up with Christ
and seated you with Me
in the heavenly realms in Christ Jesus
to show you the incomparable riches
of My grace. Surely My goodness
and love will bless you
all of the days of your life.

With extravagant blessings:
Your God

—from Psalm 121:1–2; Ephesians 2:6–7; Psalm 23:6

The pace of life can be overwhelming. So many needs and demands are placed on women that sometimes it's difficult to remember what's most important in life. We get so involved in day-to-day responsibilities that we sometimes forget the big picture.

Perhaps you feel as if you were placed on this earth to make peanut-butter sandwiches and Kool-Aid. Or that your existence is based on meeting a corporate agenda. Whatever your situation, know this: Everything you do is significant. But it isn't the checkmarks beside your "To

Do" list that prove your effectiveness. The manner in which you accomplish those tasks is what counts.

With each phone call you make and every handshake you deliver, you impact someone's life. With every face you scrub clean, your touch sends a message. Whatever your role in life, determine to let your actions communicate warmth and compassion. When every deed is done from your heart, your life is more than a title or job description. You become an effective ambassador of God's love.

God is gracious in providing not only the plan, but also the Spirit as our leader and guide. When indeed, the line is fine, God is our divine balancing pole.

Wayne Watson

Although Linda knew
her heart was in
the right place, she
couldn't shake the
nagging feeling that she
just wasn't good enough.

Doing Things Right

Linda tucked in her shirt and clipped on her earrings before surveying her reflection in the mirror. "Good enough," she said before rushing downstairs to finish getting ready for work. Halfway down the stairs she could hear the energetic buzz of her family preparing themselves for their own busy day.

"Good morning, boys!" Linda bent over the kitchen table to plant a kiss on the cheek of each of her three sons. Her oldest son, Sean, who was eleven, greeted his mother with a quick "good morning," only briefly looking up from his hand-held video game. Her younger boys—Conner, nine, and Ryan, seven—jumped up from the table to return their mother's kiss. "Good morning!" they chimed.

Grabbing a piece of toast and a small glass of orange juice, Linda began the same routine of questions she asked every morning before the boys left for school. "Did you wash your face?" "Do you have your homework?" "Did you pack your lunch money?"

Rarely did she have to send any of them back upstairs to retrieve a forgotten item. Linda was proud of how responsible her boys were. Since her husband, Mike, took an early commute to work and Linda had to get herself ready for work each morning, the boys had learned to be self-sufficient in preparing for their school day.

In spite of the hurried schedules, however, Linda felt it was important for her to be there to see the boys off to the school bus. In fact, she'd recently made it her tradition to pray with her children before they walked out the door. Each boy took a turn praying—for success on a big test or that they would do well in a soccer game or about whatever challenges

they might be facing that day. Linda always concluded the prayer time with two requests: She prayed that God would keep her children safe and that they would always act as Jesus would. This routine was special to them all.

Today's prayer seemed fairly typical until her oldest son, Sean, prayed. Linda noticed that he seemed to have a heavy heart. His eyes were closed tightly and his shoulders hunched. "Help me to do the right thing," he whispered. His words were simple, but it was obvious that much remained unsaid.

Linda ended the prayer as usual and kissed her children good-bye, all the while wishing she had time to ask Sean what was troubling him. She was perplexed with her son's petition. Was he having problems in school? With his friends? Was he in trouble? Come to think of it, he had been avoiding her lately. She was angry at herself for not having picked up on the subtle changes in his behavior earlier.

Since returning to work, Linda had found that it wasn't easy to strike a proper balance between all areas of her life.

chapter one: you are effective

With too much to do, her attention usually went to whatever clamored the loudest. Now she was beginning to see
that sometimes the most important needs just might be the
quietest.

Reflecting on the morning's prayer, Linda imagined all
the terrible problems her son might be facing. She blamed
herself for being too preoccupied to notice. It didn't take
long for seeds of doubt about her competence as a mother to
take root. Her focus turned to all the things her children
missed while she was at work. She wasn't there to greet
them when they came home from school. Rarely did they
find a meal on the table that wasn't takeout or from the
freezer. And though she did her best, it was challenging to
give each of them personal time at home.

Did her boys feel neglected or that her other responsibilities were more important to her? Was she being a good
example of a godly wife and mother? Although Linda knew
her heart was in the right place, she couldn't shake the
nagging feeling that she just wasn't good enough. What
could she do to be a better, more effective individual, wife,

and mother? Quitting her job wasn't an option because of the family's financial situation.

No matter how she turned over the situation in her mind, she couldn't find a workable solution to achieve that perfect balance. Feeling helpless, Linda did the one thing she knew she could do. She whispered her own prayer for God to help Sean make the choice that would honor Him. Still, she couldn't escape the echo in her mind of Sean's whispered plea: "Help me to do the right thing."

The workday finally over, Linda arrived home feeling weary and defeated. She was glad to see that Mike had already started heating frozen lasagna for supper. She found him reading the paper in the living room and sank into the sofa beside him. "Hey, Sweetie, how was your day?" Linda asked as she rested her head on his arm

Mike put the paper down and kissed his wife's forehead. "Fine, how was yours? You look exhausted."

Linda looked up and smiled weakly. "I am tired. It's been a long day."

13

chapter one: you are effective

Mike put his arms around her and squeezed tightly. "Well, when you feel like getting up, Sean is upstairs, and there's something he's been wanting to tell you."

Instantly the lethargic feeling that had come over Linda vanished. Her heart rate quickened in anxious anticipation of what she was about to hear. "I think I'll go on up," she said, already pulling herself out of her cozy position.

Sean's door was closed, so she knocked before entering. "Hi, Sean. Dad said you wanted to see me." She sat on the bed next to her son.

"Yeah, I wanted to tell you before you heard from my teacher," he said hesitantly.

The worst-possible scenarios raced through Linda's mind as she strained to conceal her worry and control her reaction. "OK," she said. "What's up?"

Sean took a deep breath and let it out quickly, gathering his courage, then blurted out his confession.

"Yesterday I let my friend Rusty copy my math test because he said his parents would be really mad if he got a bad grade." He paused, already feeling relieved to get things out in the open. Linda sat silently as Sean continued.

"I just couldn't believe that his parents would be so mad about a test. I felt guilty for letting him cheat, but I didn't know what else to do.

"Then I remembered how every morning you pray for us to do what Jesus would do—and yesterday, I didn't do it. So today I told the teacher what happened, even though I knew I'd get in trouble and Rusty would be mad at me. I was scared, but I just kept thinking, *I've gotta do the right thing.* Ms. Matthews gave us both a zero on the test, but she told me she was proud that I told the truth."

Sean looked up at his mother with a renewed gleam in his eyes. "I'm proud, too. I think that's what Jesus would have wanted me to do."

As Linda swallowed the lump in her throat, she hugged her son tightly. "Sean, I am more than proud right now. You've given me a special gift today. He couldn't have known how *his* triumph translated into her own, but it did.

chapter one: you are effective

Linda left the room feeling lighter than air. Suddenly the self-accusations about her ineffectiveness as a mother lost *their* effectiveness. Those negative thoughts were replaced with feelings of pride in her son and satisfaction with herself. She *was* having a positive effect on her children—she must be doing something right!

As she walked back downstairs, Linda whispered her own prayer—one of thanks that God not only was clearly guiding Sean's life but that He had taken special care to give her just the reassurance she needed as a woman on the go.

chapter two

you are needed

17

Come boldly to My throne of grace
to find mercy and grace
in your time of need.
Draw your strength from
My unlimited power.
I am able to make all grace abound to you
so that you will overflow
and have more than you need
to excel in every good work.

Empowering you,
Your God
of Strength

—from Hebrews 4:16; Philippians 4:13;
2 Corinthians 9:8

*A*ir, water, food—basic necessities of life.

We use them all day, every day, usually forgetting

to be thankful for them.

You are a basic necessity—always there for those

who need a helping hand, sound advice, a listening

ear, or a little encouragement. You're the boss, the

faithful employee, the housekeeper, chef, partner,

and childcare provider. Having a day "off" usu-

ally just means you'll be doing different work.

These are tall orders. Sometimes

they leave you exhausted. Worse yet,

sometimes you're left feeling

unappreciated—taken for granted. Others partake of your benefits every day, often forgetting to be thankful.

The things we need most are often the easiest to take for granted. Just as we would be lost without air, water, and food, if you were to disappear, those closest to you would feel lost, wondering how they'd make it.

Your presence and influence on those around you are priceless. Even when others forget to be thankful, you are important. No one can take your place. You are needed.

What a joyful thought to realize that
you are a chosen vessel for God—
perfectly suited for His use.

Joni Eareckson-Tada

Each time she failed to
reach one of the girls,
Sharon added it to the
list of reasons she
wasn't needed.

A Special Thank-You

"Good morning, this is Sharon. How may I help you?" The words rolled from her lips as they did hundreds of times a day. Finding the right balance of cheerfulness and concern was important, knowing that the caller would likely be in a very emotional state.

Sharon Davis was dedicated to her work at the pregnancy hotline center, which was a nonprofit, Christian organization. Thirty to forty hours a week, she faithfully answered calls and provided counseling to young women who were distressed by unwanted pregnancies.

The fact that the program depended on volunteer staff

made Sharon feel her contribution was that much more necessary. Her husband's lucrative career afforded Sharon the luxury of not needing to work outside the home and the benefit of investing her time in causes she felt were important.

When her two daughters entered adolescence, Sharon decided the pregnancy hotline center would be a good organization to work with. Not only would she be helping girls much like her own, but she also would convey an important message to her children about teen pregnancy.

As she waited for this caller to answer, Sharon listened to the soft sniffling of a young girl. Hoping to keep her on the line, Sharon spoke soothingly: "I can tell you're troubled. Would you like to talk about it?"

Another moment passed before the girl finally replied, "I'm pregnant." The sniffling began again.

Wanting to make her feel at ease, Sharon continued calmly. "I'm so glad you called. I'm here to help you. If you'd like, you can come to our office and talk with someone in person." She knew that some girls wanted personal counseling, while others preferred to keep everything anonymous.

"Yes, I'd like that," the girl decided. "When can I come?"

"Anytime," Sharon replied with a smile. "Just ask for Sharon."

When the call ended, Sharon said a prayer for the young girl. "Lord, please let her come." Often these young callers intended to follow through but, for one reason or another, didn't. Sharon wanted so much to show her that she had many options and that she had a heavenly Father who loved her very much.

Thirty minutes later, Sharon was pleasantly surprised to hear the voice of a young girl asking for her. As she went to the foyer to meet her visitor, Sharon recognized the teen immediately. Rhonda attended her church and was a member of her oldest daughter's sophomore high-school class. They often participated in the same church youth activities. She hoped her presence wouldn't hinder Rhonda from getting help.

Rhonda's surprised recognition of Sharon was evident. "Mrs. Davis!"

"Hello, Rhonda," Sharon said softly. "Please come in where we can talk privately."

Rhonda hesitated but then slowly followed Sharon into a counseling room.

As soon as they were seated, Sharon began, "I know you may feel uncomfortable speaking with me since you're a friend of my daughter Sara. But I want to assure you that everything we say here is confidential. You can trust me."

Rhonda nodded, unconvinced, and remained quiet. Sensing her apprehension, Sharon decided to do most of the talking until things felt more relaxed. There was plenty of information to share about the options women have when they become pregnant. Sharon wanted to emphasize that Rhonda was carrying a baby, not just a mass of tissue. She opened her Bible and showed Rhonda passages indicating that her baby was designed by God and that even if she didn't want it, it was loved.

She presented all the crisis and pregnancy information,

but Rhonda remained silent. Sharon wondered what to do next. "Rhonda, what are you feeling right now?" she asked.

Rhonda shook her head, gulping hard. "I don't know. I'm so confused! I'm scared. I don't know if I can do this!"

"Sure you can, Rhonda. You don't have to go through this alone. We at the center are here to help you." Then locking her eyes to Rhonda's, she continued, "*I'm* here to help you."

Rhonda seemed to soften for a moment, then suddenly stood up. "I have to go. I need to think about things." She reached for the door.

"Wait, Rhonda. Please call me if you need anything...before you do anything," Sharon pleaded. Rhonda looked searchingly into Sharon's eyes, then rushed out of the room.

Collapsing into her chair, Sharon prayed earnestly. "Dear Father, please protect Rhonda. Help her to remember how much she's loved and that You have a plan for her life."

Several weeks went by with no word from Rhonda. Also disappointing was the fact that she hadn't been at church in a long time. Sharon prayed daily for the troubled teen. Occasionally, she asked others at church if they had heard from Rhonda lately. It seemed that no one had. The youth minister confirmed that Rhonda hadn't participated in any youth activities in quite some time.

It was difficult for Sharon to keep from worrying that Rhonda may have done something hasty to escape her problems. *What if she has an abortion? What if she runs away? What if she tries to kill herself?* She knew that some girls feel so guilty about their situations that they take drastic measures without really considering the consequences.

Sharon's own feelings of failure to help this girl made her wonder whether her work at the hotline center was making any difference at all. As a counselor, she seldom knew what the girls decided or how their stories turned out. Sometimes it felt as if she were investing in a black hole. What did she have to offer, anyway? She had never been in their situation.

Maybe I'm too old to reach out to teenagers, Sharon thought. *Surely there are other women who would be better able to relate to these girls...*

Sharon's discouragement was aggravated by the fact that she was having trouble communicating with one of her own teenagers. Lately Sara acted aloof and uninterested in family activities. Everything Sharon tried to do to reach out to her daughter only seemed to make her pull away more. Sharon told herself that Sara was naturally trying to establish her independence, but it made her sad to feel unneeded and unwanted by her own daughter.

Convinced she was ineffective at the pregnancy hotline, Sharon decided she should find a new way to help others.

Although she believed it was time for her to leave the center, Sharon couldn't bring herself to resign until they had found a replacement. So each day she went through the motions, lacking the zeal she once had when she felt that her presence made a difference. Each time she failed to reach one of the girls, Sharon added it to the list of reasons she wasn't needed. She no longer noticed the small victories she had a hand in or the gestures of appreciation from coworkers or teens.

One morning, while taking care of unfinished paperwork,

Sharon was interrupted by a soft tap on her office door. "Come in," she replied without looking up.

As the door slowly opened, a young girl timidly peeked in. "Hi, I hope this isn't a bad time," she said questioningly. It was Rhonda.

Immediately Sharon stood to welcome her. "No, no, not at all! Please come in." As she ushered her in, Sharon couldn't help but notice the small bulge under Rhonda's oversized shirt.

Sitting down beside her, Sharon didn't know what to say first. She had so many questions. How was she feeling? Where had she been? What had she decided about the baby? Instead, Sharon simply smiled and waited for Rhonda to speak. *I don't want to blow it and scare her away like our last visit,* she thought.

"Mrs. Davis," Rhonda began, "I just wanted to stop by and say 'thank you.' When I came in here last time, I was convinced that my life was over and that there was no way out. You reminded me of truths I already knew but had for-gotten because I was so wrapped up in my own troubles. I

know that my baby deserves a chance at life, even if it isn't
with me."

Rhonda reached into her purse, pulled out a picture
frame, and tentatively handed it to Sharon. It was an ultra-
sound picture of the baby. Sharon could see every feature of
the profile. She was so moved that tears filled her eyes and
then flowed down her cheeks. "Thank you, Rhonda," she
whispered.

"If it weren't for you, I don't know what would have happened to me," the girl continued. "Although I haven't decided
whether I'm keeping the baby or giving it up for adoption, I do
know that if you hadn't been there…it would already be too
late to make that decision." Rhonda smiled and pointed to the
picture. "I just wanted you to know the impact you had on my
life and on the life inside me."

All of the worry and defeat that had weighed Sharon
down over the past several weeks seemed to melt away. As
she embraced Rhonda in a heartfelt gesture of gratitude and
relief, she realized that even if she couldn't always see the
results, she was needed.

chapter three

you are focused

Life is full of distractions.
Focus on true, noble, and right things—
purity and loveliness.
Think about everything that is admirable
and praiseworthy.
The key is fixing your eyes on Me
as you run with endurance
the race I've marked out
especially for you.
I will shower My blessings over you
as you press toward the goal
for the prize of God's
upward call in Me.

Follow Me,
Jesus—
The Author
and Finisher
of Your Faith

—from Philippians 4:8; Hebrews 12:1–2;
Philippians 3:14

I saw you the other day.

Well, it wasn't exactly you, but it reminded me of you. I was mesmerized by a clown juggling four basketballs while riding a unicycle across a tightrope. Forty feet above the ground, she kept her balance and kept the balls floating through the air as though they were weightless and the task effortless. Surely it was you under that wig and makeup.

Every day you perform a juggling act as you complete tasks for your boss, co-workers, friends, and family. Sometimes the tasks are mindless and you juggle with ease. Other times, however, someone throws in a couple of extra balls or your unicycle gets a flat. Then it takes more deliberate focus to keep everything balanced and moving.

Amazingly, you never seem to lose sight of what's important. In trials, you persevere and prevail. Despite all the distractions in life, you stay focused and keep moving toward the goal. Your "performance" is awe-inspiring. And at the end of the day, you deserve a standing ovation!

Standing firm is an act of the will.
Sometimes our emotions go along with it,
and sometimes they don't,
but it's a choice.

Dottie McDowell

Arriving home totally
worn out, Amanda
listened to the messages
on her answering machine
and heard a voice
from the past.

Life's a Race

Her heart was racing. Her lungs ached to be filled with oxygen. Sweat fell from her brow, making it difficult to see what lay ahead. Every muscle throbbed with exertion. Trees and buildings blurred as she passed them. The only sound she could hear was the thud of her shoes hitting the pavement. Though her body cried, "Stop!" she would not. Amanda Pearson loved to run.

Amanda didn't need an alarm to wake up each morning at five o'clock for her daily run. Before the sun had risen, before the noise of the day, she was out pounding the pavement.

She'd been called a fanatic—and she was. But she

needed to run. It was her special time. Time to think, to plan, with no interruptions. Time to gather herself for a day filled with demands. This was her opportunity to be alone with God.

Today would be just as busy as any other day. As a registered nurse, Amanda worked four days a week, from 7 A.M. to 7 P.M., at a local hospital. She loved her job, but it was demanding. Working alongside meticulous doctors and caring for needy patients wasn't easy. She spent twelve hours a day on her feet, running from one minor crisis to the next, with a few major ones thrown in-between.

Amanda tried to keep a good attitude, but juggling so many tasks at the same time didn't always bring out the best in her. Yesterday she caught herself using sarcasm to get her point across to another nurse. She had to admit that it wasn't the first time she had been guilty of acting grumpy when complications arose. It was something she wanted to change.

Amanda knew she probably would have to stay late to chart notes tonight, but that was becoming the norm. It

would definitely be one of those nights when she'd grab a quick bite to eat and collapse into bed, exhausted.

The day proved to be as hectic as she'd predicted. Arriving home totally worn out, Amanda listened to the messages on her answering machine and heard a voice from the past. Rachel, an old friend from high school, had left a message simply asking Amanda to return her call.

Rachel was the one who had encouraged Amanda to join the cross-country running team, despite the fact that Amanda had never run before. It seemed as though a lifetime had passed since then.

The two women lived only a few miles apart, but they hadn't kept in touch. Rachel had married and stayed at home to care for her two children, while Amanda's life revolved around her work. They had talked about getting together on a few occasions, but those plans had never materialized. Being in two different stages of life with different needs and interests, they had simply drifted apart.

The next day, Amanda called Rachel during a break at work. Her girlhood friend sounded her usual cheerful self,

and after chatting for a few minutes, she gently announced, "Amanda, I have breast cancer." Amanda was dumb-founded. Rachel had shared this information as if she were simply saying she had a pimple on her face.

"What do you mean, you have breast cancer?!" Amanda responded incredulously. "How bad is it?"

"The cancer appears to be contained, and my prognosis is good," Rachel explained. "I've been receiving radiation and chemotherapy for the past six weeks. I'm scheduled to have a complete mastectomy next week." She paused to let the news sink in. "All in all, I'm doing pretty well these days."

Suddenly Amanda's view of the world changed dramatically. Although she was confronted with illness and death every day at work, this reality hit much closer to home. It was hard to believe that someone she knew, someone her own age, could have this terrible, life-threatening disease. Amanda resolved to support her friend through this difficult time. She promised Rachel she'd stop in for a visit after work.

life's a race

Amanda had never dealt with such a crisis in her own circle of family and friends, and she was surprised at how it affected her. When she arrived at Rachel's home that evening, she was struck by the contrast of her surroundings in light of the situation. Neither the house nor the atmosphere felt bleak or dismal.

On the contrary, everything about Rachel's home conveyed a feeling of warmth, comfort, and cheer—from the budding flower beds bordering the walkway, to the bright kitchen decorated with sunflowers and cluttered with Post-It notes, to the cozy living room filled with family photos and children's trophies.

Amanda had expected to find someone sick and feeble; instead, she saw a vibrant woman full of hope and life. The only sign of Rachel's cancer was the bandanna she wore to conceal her hair loss.

"I'm having a good day," Rachel explained when Amanda commented on how energetic and upbeat she seemed. The two women unpacked the meal Amanda had brought for the family and enjoyed a small reunion. Rachel

graciously accepted her friend's offer to help out around the house and showed Amanda some of the chores that were being overlooked.

Finally it was time for Amanda to leave, and as she prepared to go, she suddenly realized that the bandanna Rachel wore looked familiar. "Is that one of the bandannas we wore in high school?" she asked, leaning closer to get a better look.

Rachel smiled warmly. "Yes, it is. I was wondering when you'd notice. The day I was diagnosed with cancer, I searched through all my high-school memorabilia, hoping it was still there. I've been keeping it in my pocket until recently. It brings back so many good memories that I like having it around."

Amanda stood in awe, reaching out to touch the knot that held the cloth tightly to Rachel's head. As if reading her thoughts, Rachel deftly untied the knot and handed the bandanna to her friend. "Just don't look at my hair right now; it's a mess!" Rachel said as she tried to cover her head with her hand.

48

life's a race

Amanda carefully examined the bandanna Rachel had worn during the four years they ran track in high school. As she opened the fold of fabric, she saw what she was looking for. Although faded, the inscribed words still bore a message of hope and endurance. Amanda ran her fingers along the floral design that used to be their "trademark," then let them rest on what was once their favorite passage of Scripture. She read it aloud:

"Hebrews 12:1—'Let us throw off everything that hinders and the sin that so easily entangles, and let us run with perseverance the race marked out for us.'"

They had chosen the verse years ago to bring inspiration and an extra measure of strength for an upcoming race. Before each meet the two friends would tie their matching bandannas on their wrists, ankles, or foreheads.

Rachel's voice brought Amanda back from her reverie. "This bandanna has helped me remember what's really important and that I can finish this race just as I have all the others."

chapter three: you are focused

Rachel's example of faith and her own fond memories touched Amanda. "Thank you for today, Rachel. You've reminded me of what I seem to be forgetting lately. Sometimes I'm so wrapped up in what's going on in my own life that I get tangled up, so to speak, and forget about the real race I'm in. I'm so glad I got to spend this time with you." Amanda said good-bye and promised to come again soon, then went straight home to search for her own bandanna.

Her encounter with Rachel had a dramatic effect on Amanda's outlook. Rather than seeing those who were ill as medical cases or statistics, she now understood that the people she cared for were individuals who mattered—someone's mother or brother or friend.

This insight gave Amanda a new focus at work. She spent more time with her patients, paying attention not only to their physical needs but to their emotional ones as well. She looked for ways to be more helpful to the doctors and her coworkers, knowing that their jobs are equally difficult.

Each day, Amanda focused on the fact that she was running a spiritual race—and the only thing she didn't have

50

time for was letting unimportant obstacles hinder her from her real goals.

Amanda's newfound compassion made her not only a better nurse but also a more purposeful runner. One specific race has become very special to her. At every opportunity, Amanda runs among thousands of others, sporting her old pink bandanna and a number on the front of her shirt. She runs to raise awareness for breast cancer. During every race she wears a sign on her back, proclaiming her inspiration for the race—"In celebration of my friend Rachel"—a dedication to a remarkable woman who is winning the battle against breast cancer and who helped Amanda to regain her focus in life.

chapter four

you are worthy

Life can sap your heart and soul.
In the midst of your hectic schedule,
I am your hiding place.
Take time to be still
and know that I am God.
Come to Me when you're worn out
and stressed out.
I'll refresh you and show you how
to live freely and lightly.
In My presence,
you'll find satisfying joy.

Filling you,
Your God
of Hope

—From Psalms 32:7; 46:10;
Matthew 11:28–30; Psalm 16:11

Ahh…relaxation…renewal. Do these words describe your condition, or do they merely conjure up fading memories? When was the last time you took a break from it all? If you can't remember, you're overdue.

Close your eyes and imagine your ideal getaway. Do you see yourself on a deserted island, penning the novel you never found time to write? Or rock climbing in the desert, feeling exhilarated as you approach the summit?

You don't need an expensive excursion to feel refreshed, but you do need an escape. Sometimes all it takes

is a change of scenery. You could find it at a park or

in your backyard. The key is finding a place where you

can think without interruption. Dream without dis-

traction. Indulge in tranquil solitude and remind your-

self that you are worthy of rest.

Your calendar is full of commitments to others.

It's time to make a date with yourself. Set aside

time to do something you love but haven't

allowed yourself the luxury of lately.

Pamper the precious soul that is

you. You deserve it!

The next time someone tries to pass you off as a cheap buy, just think about the way Jesus honors you...and smile.

Max Lucado

In the few days since

her arrival, she'd

rediscovered an inner

peace and tranquility

that she hadn't

felt in years.

The Mountaintop

The clean mountain air was fragrant with the smell of pine, and Laurie breathed deeply. It was a beautiful day. The sun was bright, and it made her feel warm all over. A small stream glistened as it flowed down the mountain. Squirrels ran busily from tree to tree, gathering nuts. Laurie sipped her coffee and, closing her eyes, strained to capture for the coming days the feeling she had at this moment.

"Why can't life always be this simple and carefree?" she whispered. It was sheer pleasure to sit on the porch alone and take in the beauty of nature around her.

Today was the last day of her week-long vacation alone in the mountains, and Laurie wasn't ready to leave. Renting this cabin had been the best decision she'd made in a long time. Her hectic job as a financial consultant was leaving her drained, and she desperately needed to get away from it all.

At the time she'd made the reservation, Laurie felt slightly guilty about spending so much time and money on herself. She could barely imagine a whole week without work. But now she dreaded going back to the "real world." Her life was full of tight deadlines and high demands. She also felt alone. Everyone at work seemed concerned only with their own job security. There was no room for true friendships. It all seemed so empty and heartless.

"Now is not the time to be thinking about work," Laurie said aloud, trying to shake the thoughts about work and stave off the anxiety and dread of going back. "I'm going to enjoy every last minute I have here."

She left her coffee on the porch and began hiking up the same path she'd taken every morning. Today she would go farther than all the other days. She wanted to reach the summit.

Her backpack contained a water jug, sack lunch, first-aid

kit, and cell phone. One could never be too prepared, even on the smallest hike in the woods. So far she had not needed to contact anyone except to let her family know she was doing fine. Her friends and family had been gracious enough to grant her request not to call unless there was an emergency. The luxury of a silent cell phone was a vacation in itself.

Laurie's pace was relaxed as she climbed the mountain, stopping often to listen to a bird or examine a work of nature. She collected interesting leaves and stones along the way. It felt good to wander aimlessly, without the pressure of time or the tug of obligation. She loved the sounds of the outdoors and relished the vibrant colors of nature. The blues, greens, and browns around her were soothing and refreshing.

Everything in this environment brought Laurie a sense of calm. *What a sharp contrast to the busy drone of city life!* she thought as she compared the two worlds. In the few days since her arrival, she'd rediscovered an inner peace and tranquility that she hadn't felt in years.

If only I could leave everything behind for good and stay in this place. She knew the idea was impossible. *What, and live off the forest, eating nuts and berries?* Laurie laughed at the notion of becoming a mountain woman and foraging for her meals.

The path became steeper, and Laurie trudged forward, helping herself up by grabbing trees and boulders along the way. The steep incline seemed to last for miles, but looking back, Laurie guessed the distance was less than a couple hundred yards.

When the path finally leveled, she stopped to take a break. Catching her breath, she steadied herself on an old stump. "Oh!" Laurie exclaimed as she took in the view around her. She had reached the top of the mountain, and the landscape was breathtaking. She could see for miles in every direction. A large lake shimmered below. An eagle floated just above the trees. In the distance, a single mountain peak still displayed remnants of its icy snowcap.

The magnificent panorama made Laurie weep. She didn't exactly understand why she was crying, except that she somehow felt unworthy to experience such beauty. Something stirred within her, and she couldn't help but sing praises to God. "Shout to the Lord all the earth, let us sing! Power and majesty, praise to the King!" She sang one of her favorite praise songs at the top of her lungs.

One song of praise led to another. Laurie laughed out loud as she reveled in the joy. She thanked God for giving her this moment and for reminding her of His awesome power and beauty.

For the next several hours, Laurie stayed at the peak of her mountain. She basked in the warmth of God's love as she prayed and meditated. As she ate her simple lunch, Laurie couldn't help but feel like royalty dining in a most splendid palace. Everything about this place made her feel happy, complete.

The sun was moving too quickly, and Laurie knew she needed to begin her trek back down the mountain before it got dark. Reluctantly, she scanned the vista one last time and wished she could bring home the scenery and the feelings she'd experienced here. Laurie felt as though she were leaving a dear friend as she slowly began descending the mountain. She dreaded the thought of replacing this joyful experience with a life of competition and busyness once she was back home. Laurie couldn't imagine how she'd be able to keep her light shining in such a dark world.

Going down the steep part of the trail was more treacherous than going up, and Laurie had difficulty slowing her momentum. Several feet from the bottom, her foot caught on a gnarly tree root, and she stumbled to the ground.

She checked to be sure she wasn't injured and found only minor scratches on her arms and legs. "Everything seems to be in the right place," she noted as she brushed off her hands and slowly pushed herself up from the ground.

As she did, a small rock lying beside the path caught her attention. She stooped down to pick up the smooth, silver-dollar-sized stone. Although it wasn't perfectly symmetrical, Laurie couldn't help but notice that the stone was unmistakably heart-shaped. She examined it closely, tracing her finger along the rounded edges. She smiled at her discovery, recognizing that it was a message.

Laurie felt sure that God placed that rock in her path for a reason. It was a sign by which she could remember her experience. Today had been a gift to remind her that she was loved by and important to God and therefore worthy of restoration.

It also was a message—a renewed commission to share God's love with others by bringing "heart" to a world that seemed cold and callous. Laurie suddenly felt peaceful about going home. She could shine a light in her small, dark corner of the universe.

Laurie tucked the symbolic stone into her pocket. This vacation had been exactly what she needed to feel restored and able to tackle once again the hectic pace of life in the corporate world. She would return refreshed, renewed, and transformed. And she would never forget her mountaintop experience!

chapter five

you are blessed

My compassions for you
are new each and every day.
From the fullness of My grace,
you receive one blessing after another.
Don't settle for mere survival.
I sent Jesus to give you abundant life.
I delight in doing far beyond
all you can ask or even dream!

Graciously,
Your God

—from Lamentations 3:22–23;
John 1:16; 10:10; Ephesians 3:20

o you feel so overwhelmed with demands and pressures that you barely know whether you're coming or going? Or are you bored with your daily routine? Either way, you're not alone.

In everyone's life, there are times when the grass looks greener on the "other side." But next time you dream about trading your demanding life for one that looks more appealing, think about this: Many people would give their eyeteeth for just a little bit of what *you* have. If you're single, you enjoy freedom. If you're a wife, you have a lifelong companion. If you're a mother, you witness the wonders of childhood.

Where you are is exactly where God wants you to be. He has placed you here for a purpose. No one else can touch the same lives you touch. Your life and calling are unique! Take a look at all the wonderful things about the life you've been given. You'll realize that through the good times and the struggles, you are blessed.

inspirational message

What a blessing when we wait on God
who knows our heart's desires,
and wants what is best for us
and for those we love!

Nancy Corbett Cole

Not sure what she would
find, Lindsey raced out
of the kitchen, screaming
and waving her arms.

Close Call

"Just a few more things, Sweetie," Lindsey promised the toddler who clung to her hip. Nearby shoppers smiled kindly as they passed the young mother maneuvering a loaded grocery cart with one arm while hanging on to her restless fifteen-month-old son, Ethan, with the other.

Lindsey had used every bargaining tool she could think of to keep her precocious toddler quiet and still. They'd already made two stops at the bakery for free cookies, and the cart was littered with several toys that would have to be given to the cashier to be reshelved later. Lindsey was out of distractions—and Ethan was out of patience.

chapter five: you are blessed

Lindsey was relieved to find an open checkout counter. She began unloading her groceries, one item at a time, shifting Ethan's twenty-five–pound frame from one hip to the other. "What a workout!" she cried, already dreading the idea of bagging her own groceries with the same slow and deliberate process. These were the days she wished she could ignore her budget and go to the more expensive grocery store that bagged the groceries, carried them out, and loaded them into the car for her. She sighed as she bagged her own groceries one-handed.

Then she noticed that her pace was holding up everyone behind her, and her stress increased. Lindsey looked at the growing line of customers waiting for her to finish. "Sorry!" she said apologetically, then continued bagging, keeping her eyes on her work so she wouldn't have to face those she was inconveniencing. She didn't look up again until she was pushing her cart out the door.

After Lindsey's ordeal in the store, loading the car seemed easy. She shifted Ethan to her other hip once more before digging out her car keys from her purse. "Thank heaven for keyless entry!" she murmured, unlocking the car doors with the push of a button. She turned on the ignition and started the cool stream of air conditioning before strapping Ethan into his car seat. As usual, he kicked and fought to be freed from the restraint. "Sorry, buddy. We're not playing around today."

Lindsey's patience was wearing thin, and she didn't have the energy to wrestle anymore. She hurriedly loaded her trunk, hoping no one else could hear her son throwing a tantrum in the backseat.

The drive home felt much longer than the fifteen minutes it took as Lindsey vacillated between ignoring her son's pleas for release and tossing toys and snacks to the backseat to pacify him. In the few minutes she was able to tune out the noise, Lindsey tried to regain her composure.

"It's been a long day, and he hasn't had a nap," she told herself. "This is not a big deal. He'll be fine once we get home." Lindsey had learned that sometimes she could steady her own nerves by reminding herself of what was true and avoiding an emotional reaction.

chapter five: you are blessed

When she finally pulled into the driveway, the sight of the garage door opening at the touch of a button brought a sigh of relief. Lindsey couldn't help but marvel at the small blessings so often taken for granted.

"We're home!" she announced to her teary-eyed, runny-nosed baby. Lindsey unstrapped Ethan first, lest he endure another minute of this misery. He immediately stopped crying and pointed at the tennis ball suspended from the garage ceiling.

"Ball!" he said with a triumphant smile on his face.

"Yes, there's the ball. You can play with it." Lindsey lowered him to the ground. Ethan waddled over to one of his favorite diversions. The ball was Lindsey's invention to make parking easier. It was tied to a string that ended at the same height as her car's bumper. When she drove into the garage and touched the ball, she knew she was in far enough. The ball also happened to be at the perfect height for Ethan to play with it, which was an added bonus.

Good, now at least I can unload groceries with two hands!

close call

Lindsey thought. She felt a small bit of freedom as she went in and out of the house, watching Ethan play happily.

With the last bag in her arm, she leaned over and scooped up Ethan to go inside. Immediately he began kicking and screaming to be put down. "Fine!" she said, in no mood for a battle. Being careful not to drop him, she loosened her grip and let him wriggle free. "You can stay while I put the groceries away, but then it's nap time!" Ethan squealed with delight as he continued his game. Lindsey turned around, feeling defeated, and headed into the kitchen to put her groceries away.

Having a direct view into the garage allowed Lindsey the luxury of working in the kitchen without Ethan tugging at her legs. She discarded the plastic sacks and for a moment considered laying her head on the counter to rest. Suddenly, she realized Ethan wasn't in view and called his name, hoping for a response.

Lindsey felt relief when she heard his jabbering and spotted him along the opposite wall where her husband's truck

would normally sit. Ethan was squatting on the ground contentedly scrutinizing the weed trimmer.

She smiled at her little boy's inquisitive nature. He was always trying to figure out how everything worked. Lindsey didn't have the heart to interrupt Ethan's fun; she would let him play for a while longer.

Lindsey turned and headed for the kitchen. But something made her stop in her tracks. Out of the corner of her eye, she saw Ethan turn his attention toward the garage door opening. In that split second, Lindsey sensed that something horrible was about to happen. Her whole body seemed to scream out, *"Do something!"*

Not sure what she would find, Lindsey raced out of the kitchen, screaming and waving her arms. As she entered the garage, her fears were confirmed. Her husband, Jake, was driving his large pickup truck straight toward their son. In those few short seconds a million thoughts ran through Lindsey's mind. She felt as if she were moving in slow motion trying to stop this imminent disaster. *You won't make*

it in time, she thought—but Lindsey gave everything she had to reach the truck before it was too late.

The tires screeched to a halt with the truck's fender touching Lindsey's chest. With wide eyes and a look of shock on his face, Jake raised his hands in the air, wanting to know what was wrong. Lindsey slowly looked down to find her little boy only inches from the huge truck tire that would have crushed every bit of life out of him. Shaking violently, she picked up Ethan and raised him above the hood to show Jake what he almost hit.

Then Lindsey began sobbing hysterically. Jake jumped from the truck and ran to his wife and child. Holding them, he felt the magnitude of the situation. Ethan's little lip quivered, not understanding what had so upset his mother.

When Lindsey finally calmed down, Jake asked, "What made you look back after you had already checked on Ethan?"

Lindsey's first impulse was to suggest that her mother's intuition had simply kicked in. But upon further consideration, she changed her mind. "I think it was more than

chapter five: you are blessed

intuition that led me to check on Ethan at that precise moment—I couldn't let go of the feeling that he was in imminent danger. I believe it was God who prompted me to check on him and God who carried me so quickly to Ethan's side."

After their near-tragic episode, Lindsey realized how trivial the day's earlier stressful events were in comparison. "It's amazing how one's perspective can change in a matter of minutes!" she exclaimed as she told Jake more about her day.

That evening, as Lindsey sat with her husband and child on the living room floor, she didn't think about housework that needed to be done or supper that had yet to be made or any of the other things that sometimes weighed her down. Instead, she reveled in the blessings she had and knew that nothing else could make her happier.

chapter six

you are selfless

In this busy life,
it's easy to feel unappreciated.
But don't lose heart in doing good.
If you persist, you'll see positive results
in My perfect time.
Through your selfless service to others,
you will be serving Me.
Even when you think I've forgotten you,
you can be confident
that I'll faithfully complete
the good work I've started in you.
Day by day,
I'm making you more like Me.

Encouragingly yours,
God

—from Galatians 6:9; Matthew 25:42–45;
Philippians 1:6

Giving comes naturally for you. You give of your time, your energy, and your resources—not because you have to but because helping others is one of your talents.

Others know this is true. You're the first person they call for assistance because you've made a habit of always being there. And you answer the call without a grumble.

Your selfless behavior is a wonderful example of how we should emulate Jesus, the most selfless person of all. He healed others' disease and pain.

He gave unconditional forgiveness and love.
He sacrificed Himself so we could be in heaven
with Him someday. He taught us how to be humble
and put others first.

It's not always convenient or easy to be someone
who is consistently helpful and generous. You often
sacrifice your own interests and needs to provide for
others. There may be times when others abuse
your generosity, as some did Jesus. Please
don't become weary in doing good—
because although you may be tired,
you will have great rewards!

Service that's fed by humility is the forgotten truth that reinvigorates life. Instead of taking from others, it gives.

Melvin Cheatham

"My girls came through
for me in a way that is
everything I imagined and
much more!"

A Special Tribute

Anne lay in bed, barely able to keep her eyes open. She felt weak and knew that she needed medical attention. Her body wasn't recovering from surgery as it should. She'd endured the same sinus procedure several times and usually felt great in less than a week. But four weeks after this last surgery, Anne still wasn't back to normal. Two weeks ago she was readmitted to the hospital because of dehydration. Now she waited as her daughter Lesli and daughter-in-law Diane prepared to take her to the hospital again.

"I think we're going to have to cancel the party," Anne whispered.

chapter six: you are selfless

"Mama, don't worry about that right now. Let's just get you to the doctor." Lesli brushed the hair from her mother's eyes. "Here, put these slippers on." *It's just like Mama to be thinking about everyone else when she should be thinking of herself,* Lesli thought. *In fact, being so active in the lives of her three children and five grandchildren has probably hindered her recovery.*

"OK, are we ready to go?" Diane asked. The two young women gingerly helped Anne out of bed and into the car.

Lesli and Diane sat in the waiting room while Anne met with the doctor. "Mom went back to work too soon," Lesli commented. "She should have taken more time off to recover."

Diane nodded in agreement. "She goes nonstop! I don't know how she does it. Between work, family, and volunteering, her body hasn't had much rest. What do you think she'll do about the party?"

"We might just have to tell Dad," Lesli said disappointedly.

Anne was planning a huge surprise party for her husband,

John, to celebrate his fiftieth birthday. Preparations had begun months earlier when she booked his favorite band for the occasion—and now the party was just three days away. Several hundred people were invited, and the catering was arranged. Decorating was the only thing left to do.

This birthday party was extra special because just a year ago, John had been diagnosed with colon cancer. After a year of treatment, John was now cancer free.

A nurse brought Anne back to the waiting room in a wheelchair but with a good report. "Other than slight dehydration, I'm just recovering slower than usual," Anne explained. "They're changing my medication, and the doctor said I need to stop doing so much." Anne offered a smile. "They're sending me home."

On the drive home the three women tried to make a decision about the party. There was no way they could continue their plans without Anne. "But I may feel better by then," Anne suggested, "so maybe we should go ahead and hope for the best."

chapter six: you are selfless

Lesli and Diane both knew that Anne was an optimist and good at acting well even when she wasn't. Still, the girls agreed that going ahead with their plans seemed the best option considering the obstacles to postponing the party. It would be difficult to reschedule the band and to reach all the guests in time to notify them of the change.

The younger women set one condition: Anne would have to stay in bed and let them do all the remaining work for the party.

"What can we do?" Diane asked.

"Well, I've been collecting pictures of John that date back to his childhood," Anne explained. "I wanted to show everyone what an impact he's had on others. It would be nice if we could think of a special way to organize and show off the photos. I want this to be a tribute to his life."

Diane and Lesli had no problems taking Anne's ideas and running with them. After some deliberation, they decided that a special scrapbook would be the ideal way to show off the photos and something John could enjoy for years to come.

The girls spent the rest of the day working feverishly to put something together. Lesli scanned original prints into the computer to make duplicates that could be cropped and enhanced. Diane made scrapbook pages out of poster board, creatively displaying the chapters of John's life. Each section was devoted to a specific interest or event.

By the end of the day, they had accomplished a lot, but there still was much more to be done—and John would be home soon. "We can keep working tonight at our own homes and come back tomorrow," Diane suggested as they gathered their materials to leave.

Lesli nodded in agreement. "See you in the morning!"

Both worked into the early morning hours, then spent most of the following day at the same hectic pace. Their few breaks were spent taking care of their own families' needs. After two days and two nights of labor, the result was impressive: A four-foot scrapbook held all the major, and some minor, events of John's life. The massive book was bound with Velcro tabs so it could be taken apart for display at the party.

Anne was speechless when she saw the enormous tribute. "I can't believe you did this! It's wonderful!" The girls smiled appreciatively, pleased at her approval.

By the next night, Anne was feeling much better. There were even moments when she forgot she was still in recovery and was caught toting one of her grandchildren around. Anne supervised the final party arrangements, which were completed quickly with the help of several family members. Balloons and streamers were hung, and tables and chairs arranged.

Excitement grew as the guests began to arrive and everyone waited for the guest of honor. When a blindfolded John entered the quieted room, he had no idea what he would find. As the blindfold came off, the band began playing "Happy Birthday." His look of surprise was unforgettable.

Anne led John to the microphone to welcome everyone.

a special tribute

"Thank you all for coming to share this special day," she began. "We're here to celebrate John's birthday and the blessing that he's with us today.

"I didn't think we'd be able to pull this party together since I've been sick for so long. I want to thank all the family members who offered assistance during my recovery after surgery to help make this celebration possible."

Anne wore a big smile, and tears glistened in her eyes. "I especially want to thank Lesli and Diane, who helped me by working day and night to get ready for this party. I had planned to put together a special display of pictures for John but was too ill. My girls came through for me and created a beautiful album that is everything I had imagined and much more! John, this is for you," Anne said, presenting him with the scrapbook. "Happy birthday."

As guests crowded around to view the display, Lesli ran to the microphone to make another announcement. "I'd like to take a moment to make one more presentation.

"While Diane and I were working to put together this

album for Daddy, we realized that the only reason we were doing this project was because Mama couldn't. We just had to make something special to let her know how much she is appreciated for always selflessly doing so much for so many."

Lesli turned to her mother. "Here is a smaller scrapbook from those who love you most—your family. We love you, Mom."

As Anne turned to receive the album, John stepped up to add one more remark. "I feel so honored that everyone has come to share in this special celebration," he said gratefully. "I thank God that He has allowed me to overcome this disease. And thank you, Anne, for making my life complete. I couldn't have done it without you." He kissed his wife tenderly.

Anne blushed, uncomfortable with the focus suddenly shifted from the guest of honor to herself. She motioned for the band to begin, and as the crowd scattered, she thanked Lesli and Diane. "You girls are too much! I can't believe you did all this in such a short time!"

The girls exchanged smiles, and Lesli responded, "We've decided that we're becoming more like you every day—we loved exerting ourselves for others!"

"Yeah," Diane added. "I think we've finally discovered what keeps you going. It really is fulfilling to selflessly serve others. I guess we're 'women on the go' in training!"

chapter seven

you are devoted

I am for you!

I've engraved you on the very palms
of My hands. When you seek Me
and My priorities first,
I'll take care of all of your needs.
Watch Me supply all of your needs
according to My endless riches in glory.

Devotedly,
Your Faithful
Heavenly Father

—from Romans 8:31; Isaiah 49:16;
Matthew 6:33; Philippians 4:19

How does she do it?"

"Where does she find the time?"

"Does she ever sleep?"

Yes, they're talking about you. You may not hear their whispers because you're too busy helping others. But if you do hear such comments, you probably shrug your shoulders and say, "It's just what I do." You never stop to consider whether to go where you're needed; you simply answer the call. Those around you see you as some kind of superwoman. In truth, you are.

You are an amazing woman created and gifted by God to minister to others. Sure, sometimes you feel drained and wonder how it all will get done or whether all the work is worth it. But even when you don't feel like it, your devotion is priceless.

For all the times your work went unnoticed, thank you. Thank you for being there when you were tired. Thank you for giving when there wasn't much left to give. Thank you for devoting your life to touching the lives of others.

Following your life purpose demands
wholesale abandon, risk, sacrifice,
and radical trust in the loving heart
of the living God.

James Emery White

Kathy held her breath,
knowing that the couple
could simply find another
realtor to handle the deal.

The Best Mom

"We'll take it," the middle-aged couple said as they beamed at Kathy. It took every ounce of will power for her to keep from jumping up and down in front of these prospective buyers. After touring the elegant four-bedroom, three-bathroom house for thirty minutes, Kathy could see why the couple had fallen in love with it. The home was a beautiful Tudor-style structure with an interior that was spacious and exquisitely decorated.

Shaking hands with her delighted customers, Kathy congratulated them on their decision. "I'll be happy to draw up the papers, and we can meet in the morning to have everything signed."

chapter seven: you are devoted

She waved as the couple drove away, and then started her own car engine. Kathy squealed with joy. "Yes! Yes! Thank You, God!" This was a great way to end a mediocre week.

Kathy had become a real estate agent three years ago when her husband left her and their two young children. The blow had come as such a terrible surprise that Kathy jumped into a career to cover her pain. Her first instinct was to protect her children not only from painful emotions but also from suffering due to financial problems. Kathy was doing everything she could to convey to her children an image of strength and courage. Most of her energy was devoted to filling the void their daddy had left behind.

Kathy thought back to the beginning of her career as a saleswoman. After being a stay-at-home mom for several years, she suddenly was thrust into the role of sole wage earner. This was quite an adjustment, made more difficult because working in sales didn't come naturally for Kathy. It took several months for her to learn how to become a career woman, but she had thrived under the pressure. Providing for her children was Kathy's first priority, and she believed that desire was the primary reason for her success.

Parking in front of Cooley Elementary School, Kathy waited for her children to file out with the hundreds of other students. She saw her younger child, Noah, first. He ran to the vehicle, dragging his backpack on the ground. "Hey, Mommy!" Noah kissed his mother breathlessly before jumping into the backseat.

"Hey, Baby! Did you see your sister?" Kathy turned around to watch Noah buckle up.

"Yes, she's talking to a boy-ee!" Noah rolled his eyes and stuck out his tongue to show his repulsion at romantic interests. Kathy giggled at her seven-year-old son and his dramatic expression.

"Oh, I see her now." She waved at Mallory through the window. Her ten-year-old waved back, grinning from ear to ear. Bouncing into the car, Mallory kissed her mother and fastened her seat belt.

"Hi, Mama! Guess what! I think Matt Parker likes me!"

  113

chapter seven: you are devoted

Trying to appear as excited as her budding adolescent, Kathy responded, "Well, of course he does. Why wouldn't he?" That reply was enough for Mallory as she looked out the window trying to catch a last glimpse of her new interest. Kathy followed the procession of cars leaving the school.

Glancing back at Mallory and Noah chatting busily in the backseat flooded Kathy with a feeling of contentment. So many nights she'd stayed up, crying and praying that her children would not be permanently damaged from the heartbreak of their parents' divorce. Often she questioned whether *she* would survive the tragedy, much less her young son and daughter.

Now, seeing them flourish and mature despite their hardships brought a lump to Kathy's throat. God was watching over them all, even when it hadn't always felt like it. A huge sense of gratitude washed over her.

"Guess what, guys," Kathy said, trying to catch her children off guard.

"What?" they chimed.

the best mom

"I know that Friday nights are our special nights to rent movies and eat popcorn, but we need to change our plans," Kathy said, peeking in the rearview mirror to catch their reaction.

The children glanced at each other, then began to protest. "But Mom! We always get to watch movies on Fridays!" Noah complained loudly.

Mallory was indignant. "Mother, why can't we have our special night?"

Kathy tried to keep a straight face. "Well, I didn't say we weren't going to have a special night. I just said we would have to change our plans. But if you don't want to eat pizza and play at the Fun Factory before we rent movies, we can just stick to our regular Friday night routine."

The reaction of her children was worth her little practical joke. Noah and Mallory both clapped and squealed in delight.

"Do you want to know why tonight is special?" Kathy asked. Both children eagerly awaited her explanation.

chapter seven: you are devoted

"Mommy sold a really big house today, so we're going to celebrate!"

It was obvious that her children were proud of their mother. They'd been so supportive and encouraging while Kathy adjusted to the working world. Ever since their dad left, any accomplishment, big or small, was reason to celebrate. It helped to remind them all that they still had many reasons to be happy.

When they arrived home, Kathy offered the kids a snack and told them to complete any unfinished homework. "Let's finish everything before we go out so we won't have to worry about assignments the whole weekend." Kathy helped Mallory with her math problems while Noah wrote out sentences.

The excitement was almost tangible as the family prepared for their evening out. While Kathy changed clothes, Mallory primped in front of the mirror and Noah bounced off the walls. He couldn't contain his enthusiasm about jumping around in the huge ball pit or playing the vast selection of video games.

the best mom

"Are we ready to go?" Kathy asked, even though the answer was obvious—Mallory and Noah were standing at the door with their jackets on. Just as she started to lock the door, Kathy heard the phone ring. "Hold on, guys, let me grab the phone really quick." Kathy heard them moan as she ran to answer the call.

"Hello?" Kathy answered while she watched her kids wait impatiently in the doorway. The call was from the couple she'd met with that morning. The children listened to their mother's side of the conversation. "Oh, you're having second thoughts?... You'd like to see the house again, tonight?..."

Disappointment shadowed both of the children's faces as Kathy tried to appease her clients. She felt her stomach tighten, weighing her options heavily. If she didn't sell this house, they wouldn't have much reason to celebrate—or the money to celebrate with. If she canceled their plans, the kids would understand, but she hated to let them down when they were so looking forward to a night of fun. She squeezed her eyes shut, listening to the couple's concerns.

Waiting for an opportunity to interject, she decided to

chapter seven: you are devoted

explain her situation and hope her clients would under-stand. "You see, tonight is a special night for my family, and it would come as a terrible disappointment to my children if we had to cancel. Is there any way we can wait until morning to revisit the house?" Kathy held her breath, knowing that the couple could simply find another realtor to handle the deal.

After a long pause and a muffled conversation on the other end of the line, the customers agreed to wait. Kathy sighed heavily before speaking, "Thank you very much. This means a lot to me. I'll see you first thing in the morning."

She hung up the phone and headed for the door. Mallory and Noah smiled and embraced their mother tightly. Noah looked up at his mother with pride in his eyes, "I knew you would say that!"

Mallory nodded, "Thanks so much, Mom, for doing that. I know you could lose the contract because of this."

"Hey, no one's gonna take our Friday nights away from us!" Kathy stated boldly as they all climbed into the car.

the best mom

As they drove and listened to their favorite CD, Kathy could just catch the sound of her children's voices in the backseat.

"Our mom is the best in the whole world!" Mallory said to her brother.

Noah nodded solemnly in agreement. "Yeah, she's the best dad, too."

Tears came to Kathy's eyes, making the road ahead blurry. She knew that she'd made the right decision to keep their date. She also knew that even if she didn't sell this house, God would take care of them.

They were going to be just fine.

How wonderful it is that
no one need wait a single moment
before starting to improve the world.

Anne Frank